Monday Macaroni and Smoked Cheese Special

Some things in this world are sacrosanct. *Monday Night Football* is one of them, but happily, the traditional macaroni and cheese casserole is not. The dynamic duo of smoky Cheddar and savory Jarlsberg makes this outstanding dish a winner. With a man-size mug of beer, a tangy tomato salad, and a slice of apple pie for dessert, Monday Night Macaroni is ideal laptop fare for the home team.

Makes Six Servings

16 ounces elbow macaroni
4 cups milk
4 tablespoons unsalted butter
6 tablespoons all-purpose flour
1 teaspoon paprika
salt and freshly ground black pepper to taste
1/4 teaspoon olive oil
6 ounces Jarlsberg cheese, grated
6 ounces smoked Cheddar cheese, grated
1 ounce fresh Parmesan cheese, shaved

Bring five quarts of water to a boil. Add the macaroni to cook for about seven minutes. Drain and rinse under cold water. Drain again, and set aside in a large bowl.

Preheat the oven to 350 degrees.

In a heavy-bottomed saucepan, bring the milk to a boil.

Melt the butter in another heavy-bottomed saucepan. Whisk in the flour to create a roux. Continue to whisk for five minutes, being careful not to let the roux brown. Remove the pan from the heat and whisk in the hot milk. Add the paprika. Season to taste with salt and pepper. Return the pan to the heat. Cook at medium temperature, whisking constantly, until the sauce thickens, about five minutes. Remove from the heat and pour over the macaroni. Toss to cover.

Transfer the macaroni into an oiled three-quart, ovenproof serving dish.

In a bowl, combine the Jarlsberg and Cheddar. Sprinkle over the macaroni to cover. A few turns of the pepper mill, a twist or two of shaved Parmesan, and into the oven it goes. Place the casserole on a baking sheet and cook for twenty minutes.

Remove the casserole from the oven and place under the broiler, about four inches from the heat. Cook for three or four minutes. The Monday Night Macaroni is done when the top is bubbling hot and the edges turn golden brown. Serve immediately.

Lean Noodle Tip: Substitute low-fat milk and low-fat cheeses for the whole varieties.

Each Lean Noodle serving contains:

- FIBER: 0.2 GRAMS • CHOLESTEROL: 65.6 MILLIGRAMS
  - FAT: 16 GRAMS

Hanoi Helper: Stovetop Clay Pot Noodles

Fen ssu are an exotic addition to your noodle repertoire. A snap to make, these cellophane or mung bean noodles are light as a feather in their dried form, expanding to hearty-size as they soak up the flavorful juices of your Asian stovetop stew. Cooked slowly to perfection in a clay pot, the tempting tastes of savory, sweet, and spicy are beautifully balanced in every succulent mouthful. Hanoi Helper is a healthy meal the Vietnamese believe will strengthen the system during the cold winter months. Your choice of beverage — tangy beer, herb-spiced tea, or creamy Vietnamese coffee.

Makes Four Servings

4 large dried black Oriental mushrooms
4 ounces *fen ssu* noodles
8 ounces firm Chinese-style tofu
3 tablespoons soy sauce
2 tablespoons oyster sauce
1/4 cup sherry
1/4 teaspoon sugar
2 cloves garlic, peeled and flattened
1 cup chicken or vegetable stock
1 tablespoon peanut oil
1/4 inch fresh ginger root, unpeeled

2 dried chili peppers, seeded and roughly chopped
3 scallions, roughly chopped
1/2 cup shredded Napa cabbage
1/2 cup fresh basil leaves, shredded
1/4 cup freshly squeezed lime juice
cilantro leaves (fresh coriander), for garnish

Place the dried mushrooms in a glass bowl and cover with warm water to rehydrate. Set aside to soak for thirty minutes.

Place the *fen ssu* noodles in a large bowl and cover with boiling water to rehydrate. Set aside to soak for thirty minutes.

Cut the tofu into one-inch cubes and set aside.

In a glass bowl, combine the soy and oyster sauces, sherry, sugar, garlic, and chicken stock. Transfer to a three-quart clay pot or covered casserole dish.

Heat the peanut oil over high temperature in a wok or heavy-bottomed sauté pan. When the oil is very hot, add the ginger root and the chilies. Quick-cook for thirty seconds, stirring constantly. Add the scallions and the cabbage. Cook, stirring, for one more minute.

Pour the piping hot mixture into the clay pot to combine with the sauce. Place on the stove, turn the heat up, and bring to a boil.

Drain the reconstituted mushrooms. Remove the stems and discard. Slice into quarters and add to the mixture boiling in the clay pot.

Drain the rehydrated noodles and add them to the clay pot. Turn down the temperature to medium-low and stir in the tofu, fresh basil, and lime juice. Cover the pot and simmer gently for thirty minutes.

Bring the clay pot to the table. Carefully remove the cover since the stew will be extremely hot. Serve immediately.

Ladle out individual portions for each guest and garnish each with a pinch of aromatic cilantro.

An inspired arrangement of bamboo placemats, napkins caught in coconut rings, and clear glass plates and service will display the Hanoi Helper perfectly.

Lean Noodle Tip: Omit the sherry. Substitute a seasoned vegetable stock for the chicken stock.

Each Lean Noodle serving contains:

- FIBER: 2.6 GRAMS • CHOLESTEROL: 0.1 MILLIGRAMS
- FAT: 7.2 GRAMS

Chilpotle Spinach Soup with Fresh Pyramid Pasta

It's the chilpotle chilies that give this tasty vegetable soup its punch. The fun pasta pyramids are a Mexican hat tip to their native origins. Making fresh pasta is not as time consuming as you might think, so enjoy the flexibility of creating a theme noodle soup for your family and friends anytime. The Chilpotle Soup goes best with a hunk of sweet cornbread, a plateful of *buñuellos,* and a brimming cup of Mexican hot chocolate.

Makes Four to Six Servings

FRESH PASTA PYRAMIDS (8 ounces)

3/4 cup all-purpose flour
1 egg
1/4 teaspoon salt
1/2 tablespoon olive oil
1/4 tablespoon lukewarm water

CHILPOTLE SPINACH SOUP

2 tablespoons vegetable oil
1 medium onion, sliced
2 garlic cloves, peeled and minced
1 large carrot, peeled and diced
1 large tomato, peeled, seeded, and roughly chopped

3 sprigs fresh thyme
6 cups chicken or vegetable stock
salt to taste
1 1/2 cups small spinach leaves
2 canned or dried chilpotle chilies, seeded and thinly
sliced
3 ounces fresh sheep cheese, crumbled
cilantro leaves (fresh coriander), for garnish
1 large lime, cut into 4 to 6 wedges

Shape the flour into a mound on a dry work surface. Keep your bag of flour close at hand as you may need extra.

Using your fist, form a wide, shallow well in the center of the flour. Break the egg into the well. Add the salt, olive oil, and water. Scramble the egg yolk lightly with a circular motion of the fork or your fingertips. Incorporate flour from the rim of the well, gradually blending with the egg. While mixing, use your free hand to prevent the rim of flour from falling into the center too quickly.

When you have incorporated all the flour from the rim into the well, form a ball with your hands. Knead the dough until it becomes soft and has lost its stickiness. Set aside.

Clean the caked dough from your hands and work surface. Dust your hands and work surface lightly with fresh flour. Place the ball of dough in the middle of the work surface. With the heel of your hand, push down firmly into the center of the dough, giving it a slight turn. Continue to knead the dough in this fashion for five minutes or until it feels very elastic and smooth and doesn't break apart.

Shape the dough back into a ball and dust it lightly with flour. Cover it in plastic wrap and let it rest at room temperature for at least twenty-five minutes.

In a large pot, heat the vegetable oil over medium-low

temperature. Add the onion, garlic, and carrot. Sauté, stirring occasionally, until the onion begins to brown, about eight to ten minutes. Add the tomato and thyme. Mix together gently to avoid breaking up the tomato pieces. Stir in the broth and season to taste with the salt. Add the spinach leaves and the chilpotle chilies. Then partially cover the soup and allow it to simmer for fifteen to twenty minutes.

While the soup is simmering, dust a clean work surface lightly with flour and center the ball of dough on it. Roll the dough out, once away from you, and then once toward you. Be careful not to put too much weight on the dough or it will tear. Rotate the dough and repeat this process, rolling, rotating, and shaping the dough into a square to create a sheet of pasta about an eighth of an inch thick.

Cut the pasta sheet into three-inch squares, using a pair of pinking shears or a perforated-edge pastry wheel. Divide each square into two triangles. Place on a plate and cover with a dish towel. Set aside.

Bring the simmering soup to a rolling boil. Add the fresh pasta. Stir with a wooden spoon for a few seconds to prevent the noodles from sticking together. Cook for two minutes. Serve immediately.

To serve, crumble a bit of sheep cheese into each soup bowl. Ladle in the soup and garnish with a pinch of cilantro. Pass the lime wedges, please!

Lean Noodle Tip: Omit the sheep cheese.

Each Lean Noodle serving contains:
- FIBER: 0.9 GRAMS • CHOLESTEROL: 46 MILLIGRAMS
- FAT: 8 GRAMS

Carnival Ribbons with Sage and Lemon on a Bed of Chard

Sensational in its simplicity, Carnival Ribbons on a Bed of Chard is nouvelle cuisine at its finest. The clear flavors of the chard against the zestily dressed noodles will surprise even the most refined palate. Pair with chilled glasses of spirited fumé blanc and bowls of fruit gazpacho as an appetizer or for dessert, the choice is yours.

Makes Four Servings

> 3 tablespoons olive oil
> 1/2 tablespoon chopped sage, or 1/2 teaspoon ground
> 2 teaspoons freshly squeezed lemon juice
> 2 teaspoons finely minced garlic
> 2 bunches young Swiss chard
> salt and freshly ground black pepper to taste
> 16 ounces fresh pasta sheets, cut into 1-inch wide strips
>   (a combination of spinach, tomato, and beet)
> freshly shaved Parmesan cheese, for garnish

In a bowl, whisk two tablespoons olive oil, sage, lemon juice, a teaspoon of garlic to make the sauce. Set aside.

Bring four quarts of water to a rapid boil.

Wash the chard and pat it dry. If the leaves measure five inches or less, they are small enough to keep whole. Otherwise, shred them roughly.

In a large skillet, heat a tablespoon of olive oil over medium-high temperature. Add a teaspoon of garlic. Cook for thirty seconds. Add the chard and toss until well coated. Cover the pan, lower the heat, and cook for three to four minutes. Stir occasionally. Uncover the pan, raise the heat slightly, and cook for one minute to evaporate the liquid. Shake the pan so the chard doesn't stick. Season with salt and pepper to taste and remove from the heat.

Boil the pasta until al dente, about a minute or two. Drain and place in a shallow bowl. Drizzle the sauce over all and toss the pasta to coat each ribbon thoroughly.

Create a Bed of Chard on each dinner plate and top with equal portions of the Carnival Ribbons. Shave several translucent curls of Parmesan on top for an elegant garnish.

To complement this tasty tangle of colors, use Fiestaware, mixed and mismatched in multicolored splendor.

Lean Noodle Tip: Omit the Parmesan cheese.

Each Lean Noodle serving contains:

- FIBER: 1.6 GRAMS • CHOLESTEROL: 137 MILLIGRAMS
  - FAT: 17.2 GRAMS

Persian Eggplant and Noodle Terrine

The beautiful aromas of cinnamon, nutmeg, and cumin will scent the air as you cook this delectable vegetable terrine. Pass bowls of herb-scented olives, cubes of freshest feta, and slivered cucumbers as an overture to this feast fit for a sultan. With a traditional *khosaf* of sun-dried fruits drenched in rosewater to follow, you'll be regaled for one thousand and one nights.

Makes Five Servings

24 ounces eggplant, sliced 1/2 inch thick
1 teaspoon salt
16 ounces lasagne
2 tablespoons olive oil
3 tablespoons peanut oil
1 large onion, finely chopped
2 cloves garlic, minced
2 medium tomatoes, peeled and chopped
2 1/2 tablespoons tomato paste
1/2 teaspoon ground cinnamon
1/2 teaspoon grated nutmeg
1/4 teaspoon ground cumin
a pinch cayenne pepper

Sprinkle the eggplant slices with a teaspoon of salt. Set aside in a colander for thirty minutes to remove the bitter flavor.

Press any excess bitter liquid from the slices, rinse them in cold water, and pat dry with a cloth or paper towel.

Bring six quarts of water to a rapid boil. Add the lasagne, stirring to keep the sheets separated, and cook about eight minutes. Drain the pasta. Brush each sheet with olive oil to prevent sticking. Set aside.

In a large skillet, heat two tablespoons of peanut oil over medium temperature. Add the onion and garlic. Cook until soft and golden, about two to three minutes. Add the eggplant and sauté. Turn frequently to lightly brown on both sides. Add a little more oil if necessary.

Stir in the chopped tomatoes, tomato paste, cinnamon, nutmeg, cumin, and cayenne pepper. Simmer until the eggplant is soft and the sauce thickens, about five minutes.

Preheat the oven to 375 degrees.

Oil a large baking dish. Line the bottom with a layer of lasagne, then a layer of eggplant. Repeat this process until you have used all of the lasagne and all of the eggplant. Finish off the terrine by drizzling some of the sauté sauce on top for extra flavor. Bake the terrine for thirty minutes.

Allow the terrine to cool for ten to fifteen minutes while you decorate each dinner plate with sprigs of fresh herbs — purple basil, delicate chervil, and flowering thyme. Center squares of the Persian Eggplant and Noodle Terrine on each plate and pass to your guests, A basket of warmed pita bread for soaking up the marvelous juices is a must!

Each serving contains:
- FIBER: 1.8 GRAMS • CHOLESTEROL: 0 MILLIGRAMS
- FAT: 14.4 GRAMS

Pasta Zhivago

The birth of the new Russia and the revival of the old Russia blend the best of both flavors in this delicious dish. The hearty whole-wheat fettuccine lends a nutty, earthy base to the complex mellowness of the caraway sauce spiked piquant with a dash of vodka. A simply dressed salad of sweet beets and lacy celery tops and an iced bottle of vodka close at hand will have your friends dancing the troika.

Makes Four Servings

1/4 cup sour cream
1/2 cup low-fat yogurt
1 teaspoon caraway seeds
1/4 teaspoon cayenne pepper
2 tablespoons olive oil
12 ounces whole-wheat fettuccine
1 medium onion, finely chopped
1/4 teaspoon salt
1/4 cup vodka
1 tablespoon finely grated lemon zest
2 tablespoons minced fresh dill, or 2 teaspoons dried

In a small bowl, mix the sour cream, yogurt, caraway seeds, cayenne pepper, and one tablespoon of olive oil to create the sauce. Set aside.

In a large pot, cook the fettuccine in four quarts of boiling water until al dente, about nine minutes.

Heat the remaining tablespoon of oil in a large, heavy-bottomed skillet over medium-high temperature. Add the onion and cook, stirring frequently, until golden brown, about five to seven minutes. Season with salt to taste. Add the vodka and continue to cook until almost all the alcohol has evaporated, about three minutes.

When the noodles are ready, drain and add them to the "drunk" onion cooking in the skillet. Toss to coat. Add the flavored sour cream sauce and toss thoroughly. Cook for one minute longer.

Arrange the Pasta Zhivago in the center of a large warmed platter. Garnish with a flurry of lemon zest and dill. A boldly patterned floral tablecloth and red square napkins set your table with a relish of the Russias.

Lean Noodle Tip: Substitute nonfat yogurt and low-fat sour cream for the whole varieties.

Each Lean Noodle serving contains:
- FIBER: 0.5 GRAMS • CHOLESTEROL: 3.8 MILLIGRAMS
- FAT: 9 GRAMS

Pasta Out of Africa

Prepare your palate for a savory safari. The wondrous Berbere Chili makes Pasta Out of Africa a one-of-a-kind culinary adventure. It's so flavorful you'll want to keep a jar on hand in the refrigerator to enhance your favorite barbecue sauces and stews. For an African-style prelude to this scrumptious blend of smoky pulses, spices, and vegetables, dress a papaya salad with lime and quench your thirst with tall glasses of icy Kenyan coffee.

Makes Four Servings

BERBERE CHILI (One Cup)

> 1/2 teaspoon ground ginger
> 1/4 teaspoon ground cardamom
> 1/4 teaspoon ground coriander
> 1/8 teaspoon ground nutmeg
> 1/8 teaspoon ground cloves
> 1/6 teaspoon ground cinnamon
> 1 tablespoon finely chopped onion
> 2 teaspoons finely chopped garlic
> 2 teaspoons salt
> 1 1/2 tablespoons red wine
> 3 tablespoons paprika

39

1 teaspoon cayenne pepper
1/4 teaspoon freshly ground black pepper
3/4 cup water
1 tablespoon olive oil, plus a little extra if necessary

PASTA OUT OF AFRICA

16 ounces buckwheat noodles
1 tablespoon olive oil
2 cups roughly chopped collard greens
1 cup cooked black-eyed peas, drained

To make the Berbere Chili, combine the ground ginger, cardamom, coriander, nutmeg, cloves, and cinnamon in a heavy-bottomed skillet. Toast the spices over a low temperature, stirring constantly, for one minute. Remove the pan from the heat and let the spices cool to room temperature.

Combine the toasted spices, onion, garlic, one teaspoon of salt, and the wine in a blender or food processor to create a smooth paste.

Toast the paprika, cayenne pepper, black pepper, and remaining teaspoon of salt in the skillet, stirring constantly, for one minute. Stir in the water, one-quarter cup at a time. Add the spice paste, stirring vigorously to combine well. Cook the mixture over the lowest possible temperature for ten to fifteen minutes.

With a rubber spatula, transfer the Berbere Chili to a lidded jar. Let the paste cool to room temperature. Dribble a tablespoon of olive oil over the top, about a quarter-inch, to seal in the flavors of the chili. Tightly covered and refrigerated, the Berbere Chili will keep for two to three months.

Bring five quarts of water to a rapid boil. Add the buckwheat noodles and cook until they are al dente, about ten minutes.

In a medium-size skillet, heat a tablespoon of olive oil over medium-high temperature. Add the collard greens and toss until they are well coated. Cover the skillet, lower the heat, and cook for three minutes, stirring occasionally. Uncover the pan, raise the heat slightly, add the black-eyed peas, and stir together for one minute. Add one-quarter of a cup of Berbere Chili. Avoid scooping up the olive oil to keep the protective seal intact. Mix all the ingredients together, cooking for one minute.

Drain the noodles. Transfer them to a glazed earthenware serving bowl. Add the vegetable chili sauce and toss well. Send the Pasta Out of Africa on a safari around your dining-room table for your guests to help themselves.

Each serving contains:

- FIBER: 2.5 GRAMS • CHOLESTEROL: 0.8 MILLIGRAMS
- FAT: 11.5 GRAMS

Pad Thai Tossed with Extra Zest

Pad Thai is the comfort food of Thailand. A familiar street-side, one-course lunch, mounds of succulent rice noodles are served up spiked with bite-size nuggets of seafood, nuts, and vegetables. The combination of textures and flavors are so delicious you will be inspired to invent your own variations. Serve a pitcher of thirst-quenching Thai iced tea and for dessert, a sinfully sweet coconut rice pudding.

Makes Six Servings

16 ounces *sen lek* noodles
3 tablespoons *nam pla* (fish sauce)
3 tablespoons soy sauce
4 tablespoons rice wine vinegar
2 tablespoons sugar
1/4 cup tomato paste
1/4 cup peanut oil
2 tablespoons minced garlic
2 teaspoons chili powder
3 eggs, lightly beaten
4 ounces medium-size shrimp, shelled and deveined
12 ounces fresh bean sprouts, rinsed and drained
5 medium-size radicchio leaves, shredded

3 scallions, tops included, finely shredded
2 tablespoons finely minced dried shrimp
1/3 cup chopped, unsalted roasted peanuts
1/4 cup chopped cilantro leaves (fresh coriander)
2 tablespoons lime zest
4 lime wedges, for garnish

Place the rice noodles in a large bowl. Cover with hot water and let them soak to rehydrate, about fifteen minutes. Drain the noodles and set them aside.

In a small glass or ceramic bowl, combine the *nam pla,* soy sauce, vinegar, sugar, and tomato paste. Set aside.

In a wok or large sauté pan, heat the oil over high temperature. Add the minced garlic and chili. Cook, stirring constantly, for one minute. Add the noodles and the nam pla mixture and toss together. Cook for about thirty seconds to coat the noodles. Move the noodles to the side and add the eggs. Cook the eggs to set slightly, then add the noodles and scramble together. Add the fresh shrimp and scramble them into the mix. When the shrimp turn pink, add half the bean sprouts, half the radicchio, the scallions, the dried shrimp, and the peanuts. Mix together, continuing to cook for several minutes. Remove from the heat and transfer to a large platter. Scatter cilantro and lime zest on top and toss gently.

To serve the Pad Thai Tossed with Extra Zest in the traditional Thai manner, place the remaining bean sprouts, radicchio leaves, and lime wedges into small bowls within easy reach. Your guests will help themselves to a generous portion of the noodles, topping them with bean sprouts and the radicchio. A squeeze of lime adds a final zesty zinger.

Serve immediately.

Lean Noodle Tip: Omit the eggs. Reduce the peanut oil and roasted peanuts to three tablespoons and two tablespoons respectively.

Each Lean Noodle serving contains:
- FIBER: 1.2 GRAMS • CHOLESTEROL: 35.4 MILLIGRAMS
- FAT: 14.2 GRAMS

Rasta Pasta Jumped in Okra, Shrimp, and Hot Chilies

"Jamaica this yourself?" will be the question on everyone's lips when you serve this lively Caribbean-style pasta gumbo. Rasta Pasta features the unique flavors and classic ingredients that make island cuisine so special. It's a visual virtuoso. Served smartly with platters of the juiciest tropical fruits and brightened with piña colada cocktails, Rasta Pasta will lend a reggae beat to "Auld Lang Syne."

Makes Four Servings

1 1/2 teaspoons dried onion flakes
1 1/2 teaspoons onion powder
1 teaspoon ground thyme
1 teaspoon salt
1/2 teaspoon ground allspice
1/8 teaspoon ground nutmeg
1/8 teaspoon ground cinnamon
1 teaspoon sugar
1/2 teaspoon coarsely ground black pepper
1 teaspoon cayenne pepper
1 teaspoon dried chives
16 ounces medium shrimp, shelled and deveined
4 tablespoons olive oil
16 small okra, washed and trimmed

1 teaspoon fresh-squeezed lemon juice
1 red bell pepper, seeded and cut into strips 3 inches
   long by 1/4 inch wide
25 to 30 cherry tomatoes, cut in half
8 ounces long fusilli noodles
1 teaspoon minced hot Jamaican chilies (or jalapeño
   or serrano)
1/2 cup freshly squeezed lime juice

In a small bowl, mix the onion flakes, onion powder, thyme, salt, allspice, nutmeg, cinnamon, sugar, black and cayenne peppers, and chives to make a classic jerk seasoning.

Brush the shrimp with two tablespoons of olive oil. Toss them, a few at a time, in the jerk seasoning to coat each thoroughly. Shake gently to remove any excess spice. Set the shrimp aside on a baking sheet.

Bring two quarts of water to a boil. Trim the stem ends off the okra carefully, to avoid cutting into the pod. Drop the okra into the boiling water. Add the lemon juice, lower the temperature, and simmer until just tender, five to six minutes. Drain them at once and set aside.

Bring four quarts of water to a boil. Add the fusilli and cook until al dente, about ten to twelve minutes.

Preheat the broiler.

Heat the remaining two tablespoons of olive oil in a large skillet over moderate temperature. When the oil is hot, add the red pepper, tomatoes, and chilies. If the powerful Jamaican chilies are not available, substitute serrano or jalapeño. Sauté for five minutes. Add the okra, stir to combine, and reduce the temperature to low.

Place the shrimp under the broiler. Cook until they turn pink, about one to two minutes on each side. The shrimps cook quickly, so keep an eye on them to avoid overcooking.

Drain the fusilli and arrange on a large, oval serving platter. Gently toss in the lime juice. Spoon the sautéed vegetables into the center of the noodles. Fan the jerk-spiced shrimp artfully around the edges to give your presentation a crowning touch.

Each serving contains:

- FIBER: 2.5 GRAMS • CHOLESTEROL: 172 MILLIGRAMS
- FAT: 16.9 GRAMS

Pearl's Pasta Pancakes Spiced with Sauce Rémoulade

One dollop of this rich and tangy Creole condiment on top of the crisp and crunchy noodle pancake won't be enough for your Mardi Gras guests. Spread your buffet with a culinary carnival: a salad of mustard and dandelion greens, mint julep ice, and a centerpiece of Pearl's Pasta Pancakes surrounded by little dishes of the jewel-like garnishes. Glasses of pink lemonade spiked with bourbon will keep your party pulsing with a Zydeco beat.

Makes Four Pancakes (Serves Four)

16 ounces capellini noodles
1/2 cup vegetable oil
2 large tomatoes, peeled, seeded, and coarsely
    chopped, for garnish
1/2 cup cooked corn kernels, for garnish
1/4 cup finely chopped scallion, green tops included
Sauce Rémoulade (recipe follows)

Boil the capellini in four quarts of water until al dente, about one minute. Drain the noodles, rinse in cold water, and drain them again thoroughly.

Preheat the oven to 150 degrees (or turn it to the "warm" setting).

In a six-inch skillet over medium-high temperature, heat two tablespoons of oil. When the oil is hot, add a quarter of the cooked capellini. Spread the noodles evenly over the bottom of the pan, patting them down gently to form a pancake. Cook until the bottom becomes golden brown and forms a crust, about three to four minutes. Turn the pancake over and brown the other side. When both sides are crisp, place the pancake on a platter and keep it warm in the oven while you cook the other three. Repeat this process to cook the other pancakes.

Present the pancakes buffet style or, if you prefer to serve individual portions, place each pancake on a plate and garnish each separately with a colorful sprinkle of chopped tomato, corn kernels, and scallion. Either way, pass the bowl of piquant Sauce Rémoulade around the table for everyone to help themselves to a generous dollop.

Lean Noodle Tip: Substitute the egg yolk and the vegetable oil in the sauce with one-quarter cup of nonfat yogurt.

Each Lean Noodle serving contains:
- FIBER: 1.2 GRAMS • CHOLESTEROL: 0.2 MILLIGRAMS
- FAT: 30 GRAMS

Sauce Rémoulade

Makes Half A Cup

1 egg yolk
2 tablespoons vegetable oil
1/4 cup finely chopped celery
1/4 cup finely chopped scallion, green tops included
1/4 cup chopped fresh parsley

2 tablespoons prepared horseradish
1/4 lemon, seeded
1 tablespoon Creole mustard
1 tablespoon catsup
1 tablespoon Worcestershire sauce
1/2 tablespoon prepared mustard
1/2 tablespoon cider vinegar
1/2 tablespoon Tabasco sauce
1/2 tablespoon minced garlic
1 tablespoon paprika
1/2 teaspoon salt

In a blender or food processor, beat the egg yolk for one minute. With the machine running, add the vegetable oil in a thin, steady stream. Keep the machine running and add the celery, scallion, parsley, horseradish, lemon, Creole mustard, catsup, Worcestershire sauce, prepared mustard, vinegar, Tabasco, garlic, paprika, and salt. After about a minute, all of the ingredients will be thoroughly blended. Transfer to a ceramic serving bowl and set aside at room temperature.

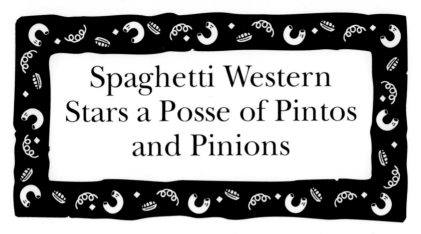

Spaghetti Western Stars a Posse of Pintos and Pinions

Round up your hungry hordes for a hearty supper Western style. The ancho chilies give each mouthful of Spaghetti Western pasta its delicious campfire flavor, and the toasted pine nuts its regional integrity. A glass of sun tea, a salad of fresh garden greens, and a whiskey-spiked fruit compote prove that we cowboys make better spaghetti than Italians do Westerns.

Makes Five Servings

1 tablespoon olive oil
12 medium cloves garlic, peeled
3 ancho chilies
2 tablespoons chicken or vegetable stock
4 medium tomatoes, peeled, seeded, and chopped
1 cup fresh corn kernels
1 cup pinto beans, cooked and drained
salt and freshly ground black pepper to taste
16 ounces spaghetti
1/3 cup pinions (pine nuts), toasted, for garnish
1/4 cup cilantro leaves (fresh coriander), for garnish

In a large pot, bring four quarts of water to a boil.

Heat the olive oil in a medium skillet over low temperature. Add the garlic cloves and cook until soft and lightly golden, about fifteen minutes. Be careful not to let the garlic burn.

Soak the chilies in hot water to rehydrate. After they are softened, make a lengthwise slit and rinse under running water to wash away the seeds. Lay them out on a flat surface. Carefully scrape the insides into a small bowl and discard the skins. Mix the chicken stock into the pulp. Set aside. For an extra zinger, soak another chili and repeat the process.

Add the chili mixture to the softened garlic in the skillet. With the back of a wooden spoon, mash together to form a paste. Cook for a minute longer. Add the tomatoes. Raise the temperature to medium-low and cook for ten minutes. Add the corn kernels and pinto beans. Season with salt and freshly ground black pepper to taste. Cook for one or two minutes longer.

Add the spaghetti to the boiling water and cook until al dente, about eight to ten minutes.

Drain the spaghetti and transfer it to a warmed earthenware bowl, both large and deep. Toss in the robust tomato sauce. Scatter the garnishes of toasted pinions and cilantro over all.

Set the stage with a red and white checkered tablecloth, bandanas folded for napkins, and a horseshoe for luck under each person's chair.

Lean Noodle Tip: Omit the pinions.

Each Lean Noodle serving contains:
- FIBER: 2.1 GRAMS • CHOLESTEROL: 0.1 MILLIGRAMS
- FAT: 4.7 GRAMS

Emperor's Garden Sesame Noodles

This is surely the most-flavored national noodle dish of China. Food lovers everywhere agree that its spicy-richness is hard to top for goodness. The preparation time is definitely fast track. The *lo mein* noodles take a minute at the most to cook. Crunchy, colorful vegetables topped with a bitter bite of scallion are instant gratification, Chinese style!

Makes Four Servings

4 scallions, for floret garnish
8 thin asparagus spears, trimmed
3 tablespoons light soy sauce
2 tablespoons dry sherry
2 tablespoons rice vinegar
1 tablespoon Oriental sesame oil
1 tablespoon brown sugar
1/2 teaspoon chili sauce
1/4 teaspoon ground Shichuan peppercorns
1 tablespoon grated orange zest
1/4 cup sesame seeds, toasted
4 medium-size iceberg lettuce leaves, rinsed and
   dried
2 tablespoons peanut oil
1 tablespoon finely minced garlic

56

16 ounces fresh *lo mein* noodles
1 large carrot, peeled and cut into matchstick-size
    pieces
1 large English cucumber, peeled, seeded, and cut
    into matchstick-size pieces

Trim the scallions, leaving the white bulb and a couple of inches of the green tops. Vertically cut each scallion into shreds, measuring an eighth of an inch wide by three inches long. Place the pieces into a small bowl of ice water. After ten to fifteen minutes, the scallions will form tight curls. Set aside.

Bring one quart of water to a boil in a medium saucepan. Add the asparagus and cook for three minutes. Drain and rinse in cold running water. Slice the asparagus on an angle into pieces, measuring one and one-half inches long. Set aside.

In a large pot, bring five quarts of water to a boil.

In a glass bowl, combine the soy sauce, sherry, rice vinegar, sesame oil, brown sugar, chili sauce, peppercorns, orange zest, and toasted sesame seeds. Stir well and set aside.

From here on in, you will be working quickly. Place a lettuce leaf in the bottom of each serving bowl. Chinese celadon bowls are a perfect choice for prettily presenting this dish. Place three or four ice cubes in another matching bowl. Drain the scallion florets and lay them on top of the ice cubes to keep them perky. Arrange the bowls on a lacquer serving tray and set aside.

In a wok or large sauté pan, heat the peanut oil over medium-high temperature. Add the minced garlic and sauté for one minute. Add the soy sauce mixture and bring it almost to a boil. Remove the wok from the heat.

Plunge the lo mein into rapidly boiling water. Cook about one minute. Drain the noodles and pour them into the wok.

Toss thoroughly to coat. Transfer to a large celadon serving bowl.

Compose the slices of asparagus, carrot, and cucumber in an attractive pattern over the lo mein. To insure the crispness of the vegetables, wait and toss them into the noodles just before serving. Place the bowl of lo mein on the serving tray and you are ready to serve.

Nestle equal portions of the Emperor's Garden Sesame Noodles in the lettuce cups. Scatter some curly scallion florets over each succulent portion.

To create a lovely table setting, float a single water lily or gardenia in a glass bowl as your centerpiece. Since red is the color of good fortune in China, contrast the white of the blossom with shimmering scarlet candlelight, red napkins, and matching tablecloth.

Lean Noodle Tip: Reduce the amount of sesame oil to one teaspoon, the sesame seeds to two tablespoons, and the peanut oil to one tablespoon.

Each Lean Noodle serving contains:

- FIBER: 1.2 GRAMS • CHOLESTEROL: 0 MILLIGRAMS
- FAT: 10.7 GRAMS

Jewel in the Crown Sweet and Savory Noodles

Charm the guests at your next dinner party with this exotic creation. A perfect pair of Indian-spiced noodles presented side by side in a single exquisite entree. One is sweetened with gingered vegetables and shredded coconut. Its savory partner is flavored with turmeric and a pinch of asafetida, the pungent spice reminiscent of fresh truffles. Offer a fruity red wine to complement and an assortment of tiny samosas to tantalize.

Makes Six Servings

SWEET NOODLES

> 8 ounces rice noodles
> 2 teaspoons black mustard seeds
> 1 tablespoon white gram beans
> 1 tablespoon grated fresh ginger
> 2 fresh green chilies, seeded and minced
> 1/4 cup grated carrot
> 1/2 cup green peas, cooked
> 2 tablespoons peanut oil
> 1 teaspoon salt
> 1/4 cup shredded coconut
> 1 lemon, thinly sliced, for garnish

SAVORY NOODLES

  8 ounces rice noodles
  2 teaspoons black mustard seeds
  1 tablespoon white gram beans
  2 dried red chilies, seeded and minced
  1/4 teaspoon ground asafetida
  1/4 teaspoon turmeric
  1/4 cup water
  2 tablespoons peanut oil
  1 teaspoon salt
  1/4 cup coarsely chopped cilantro leaves (fresh
     coriander)
  1/2 teaspoon finely grated lemon zest
  juice of one lemon
  1/4 cup shredded coconut, for garnish
  seeds of one pomegranate, for garnish

Prepare the rice noodles for both recipes. Bring six quarts of water to a boil in a deep pot. Turn off the heat and add all the noodles to the pot. Soak for five minutes to rehydrate. Drain and rinse immediately under cold water to prevent sticking. Transfer them to a large bowl or platter. Set aside.

Preheat the oven to 150 degrees, or the lowest setting.

To prepare the Sweet Noodles: On a large plate, arrange the mustard seeds, gram beans, fresh ginger, green chilies, grated carrot, and the green peas. Keep the plate right next to the stove so you can work quickly.

Heat the peanut oil in a large skillet over high temperature. When the oil is very hot, reduce the temperature to medium-high and add the mustard seeds. As soon as they begin to sputter, add the gram beans and cook, stirring, until light brown. Mix in the ginger and chilies. Cook for ten to fifteen seconds. Add the carrots and peas. Cook for two minutes longer, stirring constantly. Add half the noodles and toss. Season with salt. Sauté for a minute or two. Sprinkle in a quarter cup of coconut and cook for one more minute.

Transfer the Sweet Noodles to a platter. Place in the oven to warm while you prepare the Savory Noodles.

Once again, arrange your ingredients on a large plate: the mustard seeds, gram beans, red chilies, and ground asafetida. Place the plate next to the stove for easy access.

Dissolve the turmeric in a quarter cup of water. Set aside.

Heat the peanut oil in the skillet over high temperature. When the oil is very hot, reduce the temperature to medium-high and add the mustard seeds. When they begin to sputter, add the gram beans. Cook until golden. Add the minced chilies and asafetida. Sauté about one minute until the beans begin to darken. Add the rest of the noodles, immediately followed by the turmeric and the salt. Toss the noodles to coat thoroughly with the spices. Continue cooking for four or five minutes. Turn off the heat and add the cilantro, the lemon zest, and lemon juice. Toss well.

The Sweet and Savory Noodles are at their most dazzling presented on the same large platter. Arrange the Sweet Noodles down the left side of your serving dish and decorate them with the translucent slices of lemon. Arrange the Savory Noodles down the right side of the platter and garnish with the shredded coconut. Where sweet and savory touch, lay a jewel-like chain of pomegranate seeds — the crowning glory to this gem of a dish.

Each serving contains:
- FIBER: 1.6 GRAMS • CHOLESTEROL: 0 MILLIGRAMS
- FAT: 13.9 GRAMS

NOODLE INDEX